The 100 Word Exercise Book

Greek

Second edition

Series concept: Jane Wightwick
Greek edition: Ioanna Psalti

g-and-W
PUBLISHING

Published by *g-and-w* PUBLISHING
47a High Street
Chinnor
Oxfordshire OX39 4DJ

Second edition, books and audio CD

© *g-and-w* PUBLISHING 2008

ISBN 978-1-903103-20-3

Designed by: Robert Bowers

Illustrated by: Mahmoud Gaafar

Available in the series:
Arabic
Chinese
Greek
Gujarati
Hindi
Japanese
Panjabi
Russian
Urdu

Printed in China
by WKT Co. Ltd.

1 2 3 4 5 6 7 8 9   15 14 13 12 11 10 09 08

◎ Contents

Flashcards (8 sheets of tear-out topic flashcards)

◎ INTRODUCTION

In this activity book you'll find 100 key words for you to learn to read in Greek. All of the activities are designed specifically for reading non-Latin script languages. Many of the activities are inspired by the kind of games used to teach children to read their own language: flashcards, matching games, memory games, joining exercises, etc. This is not only a more effective method of learning to read a new script, but also much more fun.

We've included a **Scriptbreaker** to get you started. This is a friendly introduction to the Greek script that will give you tips on how to remember the letters.

Then you can move on to the 8 **Topics**. Each topic presents essential words in large type. There is also a pronunciation guide so you know how to say the words. These words are also featured in the tear-out **Flashcard** section at the back of the book. When you've mastered the words, you can go on to try out the activities and games for that topic.

There's also a **Round-up** section to review all your new words and the **Answers** to all the activities to check yourself.

Follow this 4-step plan for maximum success:

1 Have a look at the key topic words with their pictures. Then tear out the flashcards and shuffle them. Put them Greek side up. Try to remember what the word means and turn the card over to check with the English. When you can do this, cover the pronunciation and try to say the word and remember the meaning by looking at the Greek script only.

2 Put the cards English side up and try to say the Greek word. Try the cards again each day both ways around. (When you can remember a card for 7 days in a row, you can file it!)

3 Try out the activities and games for each topic. This will reinforce your recognition of the key words.

4 After you have covered all the topics, you can try the activities in the Round-up section to test your knowledge of all the Greek words in the book. You can also try shuffling all the flashcards together to see how many you can remember.

This flexible and fun way of reading your first words in Greek should give you a head start whether you're learning at home or in a group.

◎ SCRIPTBREAKER

The purpose of this Scriptbreaker is to introduce you to the Greek script and how it is formed. You should not try to memorise the alphabet at this stage, nor try to write the letters yourself. Instead, have a quick look through this section and then move on to the topics, glancing back if you want to work out the letters in a particular word. Remember, though, that recognizing the whole shape of the word in an unfamiliar script is just as important as knowing how it is made up. Using this method you will have a much more instinctive recall of vocabulary and will gain the confidence to expand your knowledge in other directions.

The Greek script is not nearly as difficult as it might seem at first glance. There are many letters that are the same as the English ones, there are capital letters, and, unlike English, words are usually spelled as they sound:

- Greek spelling and pronunciation are much more systematic than in English
- You will recognise some of the letters straight away, but beware of false friends!

◎ The alphabet

There are 24 letters in the Greek alphabet. A good way of learning the alphabet is to take it in three stages.

Stage 1

The first group consists of 10 letters which look and sound like their English equivalents – but watch out for lower case Z (ζ) and M (μ).

The first 8 are :

Capital letter:	A	E	Z	I	K	M	O	T
Lower case:	α	ε	ζ	ι	κ	μ	ο	τ
Pronunciation:	a	e	z	i	k	m	o	t

The next two letters are misleading as they resemble English letters but are not exact equivalents:

Capital letter:	N	Y
Lower case:	ν	υ
Pronunciation:	n	i

We can now use these letters to make a word:

μάτι   *mati*   eye

✔ Greek has 24 letters
✔ Some letters are like their English equivalents
✔ Some look like English, but are **false friends**

Stage 2

This stage consists of letters which resemble the English letters as capitals and/or lower case but they are tricky as they represent totally different sounds. These are called "false friends".

Capital letter:	B	H	P	X
Lower case:	β	η	ρ	χ
Pronunciation:	*v*	*i*	*r*	*h* (hard)

We can use these letters to make some more words

χέρι	<u>*heri*</u>	hand
μικρό	<u>mi*kro*</u>	small
μύτη	<u>mi*ti*</u>	nose

✔ There are four false friends:

B, β = *v*   H, η = *i*   P, ρ = *r*   X, χ = *h*

Stage 3

Here you will find all the letters which have unfamiliar shapes, although most of them represent sounds familiar to an English-speaker.

The first four letters represent sounds which in English are made by putting two letters together.

Capital letter:	Δ	Θ	Ξ	Ψ
Lower case:	δ	θ	ξ	ψ
Pronunciation:	*TH*	*th*	*ks*	*ps*

6

Now look at these words:

ψάρι	_psari_	fish
ταξί	_ta<u>ksi</u>_	taxi

The next five letters are:

Capital letter:	Φ	Λ	Π	Σ	Ω
Lower case:	φ	λ	π	σ, ς*	ω
Pronunciation :	_f_	_l_	_p_	_s_	_o_

*The form of this letter depends on its position in a word. **ς** is only used at the end of a word, otherwise **σ** is used, e.g. **σκύλος** (skilos) – dog.

Pay particular attention to **Γ γ** (gh) which has two possible pronunciations (see page 8).

For example:

γάτα	_<u>gh</u>ata_	cat
μεγάλο	_me<u>gh</u>alo_	big

Note also that a Greek question mark looks like an English semi-colon:

πόσο;	_poso?_	how much?

- ✔ Most Greek letters represent sounds similar to English
- ✔ There are four letters representing sounds which in English are made by putting two letters together:

  Δ, δ (_TH_)   Θ, θ (_th_)   Ξ, ξ (_ks_)   Ψ, ψ (_ps_)

◎ Masculine, feminine, and neuter

In English, the definite article is always "the", e.g. "the sofa", "the cat", "the taxi". In Greek, nouns are either masculine (ο καναπές, _o kana<u>pes</u>_, "the sofa"), feminine (η γάτα, _i <u>gh</u>ata_, "the cat") or neuter (το ταξί, _to ta<u>ksi</u>_, "the taxi") and the word for "the" varies accordingly. There is also one example of a plural "the": τα μαλλιά _ta ma<u>lia</u>_, "hair" (literally "hairs"). It is important as you progress in Greek to know whether a word is masculine, feminine or neuter and, for this reason, we have given the 100 words with their articles. Try to learn new words this way – it will help you later.

◎ Pronunciation tips

Greek is probably one of the easiest languages to read as what you see is generally what you hear. The Greek used today is very much simplified. The once prolific stress and breathing marks have been reduced to only one small mark above a vowel (e.g. ὁ) which indicates where the stress falls on a word (shown in the pronunciation by underlining).

The Greek vowels have simple pronunciations:

A, α   always pronounced "a" as in "bat"
E, ε   always pronounced "e" as in "bed"
I, ι / Y, υ / H, η   all pronounced "i" as in "tin"
O, o / Ω, ω   both pronounced "o" as in "pot"

A combination of two vowels may produce a different sound. Use the pronunciation guide for the individual words to help you. Note these especially:

αυ   pronounced "af" or "av", e.g. αυτοκίνητο (*aftokinito*) – "car"; αὐριο (*avrio*) – "tomorrow"

ευ   pronounced "ef" or "ev", e.g. ευχαριστώ (*efharisto*) – "thank you"

Many of the other Greek letters are pronounced in a similar way to their English equivalents, but here are a few points to note:

P, ρ   pronounced trilled as the Scottish "r" at of the front of the mouth

X, χ   pronounced like the "ch" in the Yiddish "chutzpah"

Γ, γ   pronounced either as "g" as in "gate" or "y" as in "yes"

◎ Summary of the Greek alphabet

The table below shows all the Greek letters, both capitals and lower case. You can refer to it as you work your way through the topics.

A	α	*a*	I	ι	*i*	P	ρ	*r*	
B	β	*v*	K	κ	*k*	Σ	σ ς	*s*	
Γ	γ	*gh*	Λ	λ	*l*	T	τ	*t*	
Δ	δ	*TH* (as in "that")	M	μ	*m*	Y	υ	*i*	
E	ε	*e*	N	ν	*n*	Φ	φ	*f*	
Z	ζ	*z*	Ξ	ξ	*ks*	X	χ	*h*	
H	η	*i*	O	o	*o*	Ψ	ψ	*ps*	
Θ	θ	*th* (as in "thin")	Π	π	*p*	Ω	ω	*o*	

① AROUND THE HOME

Look at the pictures of things you might find in a house.
Tear out the flashcards for this topic.
Follow steps 1 and 2 of the plan in the introduction.

το τραπέζι
to trapezi

η τηλεόραση
i tileorasi

το παράθυρο
to parathiro

η καρέκλα
i karekla

ο υπολογιστής
o ipologhistis

το τηλέφωνο
to tilefono

ο καναπές
o kanapes

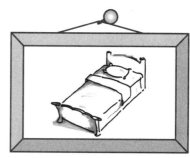

το κρεβάτι
to krevati

το ψυγείο
to psiyio

το ντουλάπι
to doolapi

ο φούρνος
o foornos

η πόρτα
i porta

◎ **M**atch the pictures with the words, as in the example.

καναπές

κρεβάτι

παράθυρο

τραπέζι

τηλεόραση

υπολογιστής

τηλέφωνο

καρέκλα

◎ **N**ow match the Greek household words to the English.

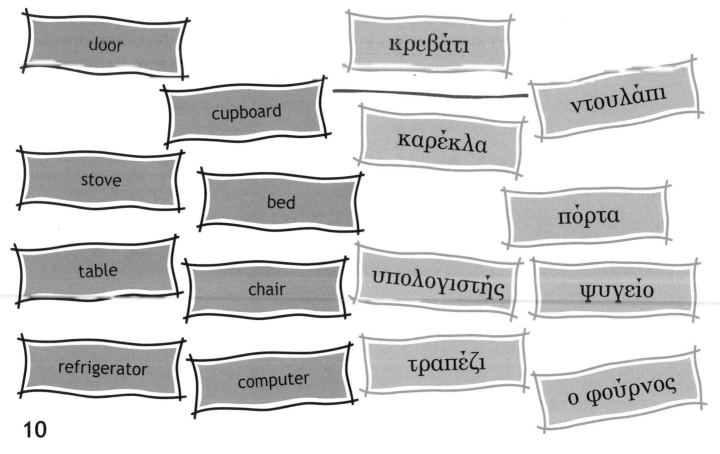

◎ Match the words and their pronunciation.

τραπέζι

ντουλάπι

υπολογιστής

κρεβάτι

παράθυρο

τηλέφωνο

τηλεόραση

καρέκλα

parathiro

krevati

tilefono

karekla

tileorasi

trapezi

ipologhistis

doolapi

◎ See if you can find these words in the word square.

The words can run left to right, or top to bottom:

φούρνος

κρεβάτι

καρέκλα

ψυγείο

πόρτα

καναπές

η	κ	α	ρ	έ	κ	λ	α
κ	τ	θ	μ	τ	π	σ	φ
ρ	κ	ψ	υ	γ	ε	ι	ο
ε	φ	π	ν	ρ	ν	α	ύ
β	ξ	ό	ν	ι	δ	γ	ρ
ά	κ	ρ	ε	β	ς	ψ	ν
τ	υ	τ	μ	φ	ω	ω	ο
ι	κ	α	ν	α	π	έ	ς

11

Decide where the household items should go. Then write the correct number in the picture, as in the example.

1. τραπέζι   2. καρέκλα   3. καναπές   4. τηλεόραση
5. τηλέφωνο   6. κρεβάτι   7. ντουλάπι   8. φούρνος
9. ψυγείο   10. υπολογιστής   11. παράθυρο   12. πόρτα

Now see if you can fill in the household word at the bottom of the page by choosing the correct Greek.

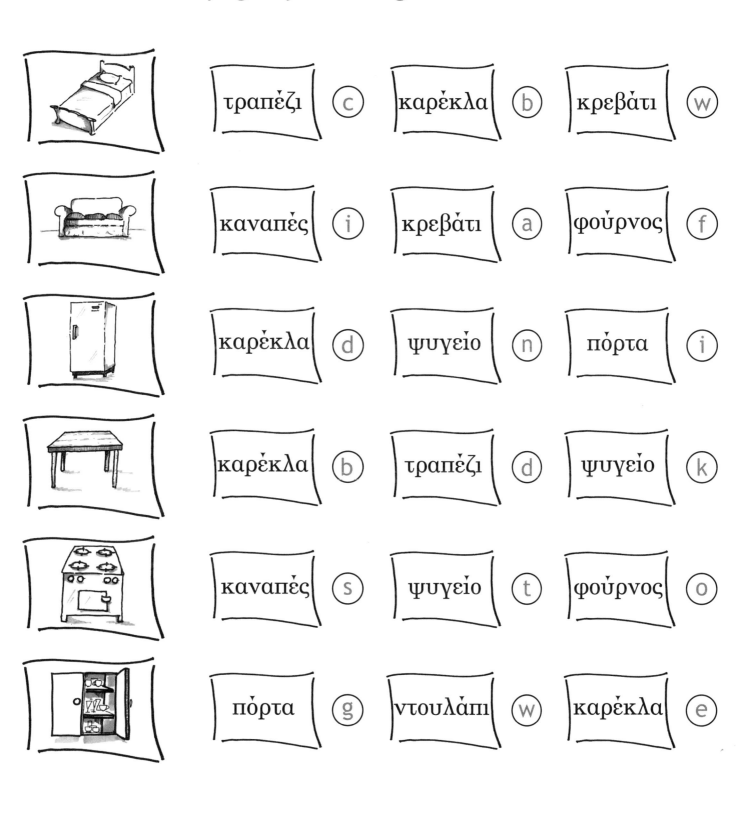

English word: ⓦ ○ ○ ○ ○ ○

② CLOTHES

Look at the pictures of different clothes.
Tear out the flashcards for this topic.
Follow steps 1 and 2 of the plan in the introduction.

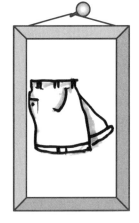

η ζώνη
i zoni

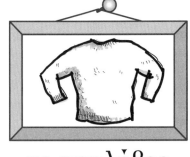

το πουλόβερ
to poolover

το αθλητικό
φανελλάκι
to athlitiko fanelaki

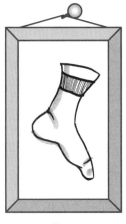

η κάλτσα
i kaltsa

το σορτς
to sorts

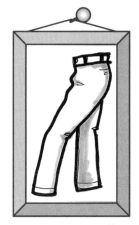

το παντελόνι
to pandeloni

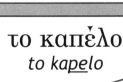

το καπέλο
to kapelo

το επανωφόρι
to epanofori

η φούστα
i foosta

το φόρεμα
to forema

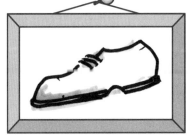

το παπούτσι
to papootsi

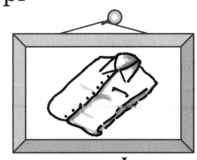

το πουκάμισο
to pookamiso

◎ **M**atch the Greek words and their pronunciation.

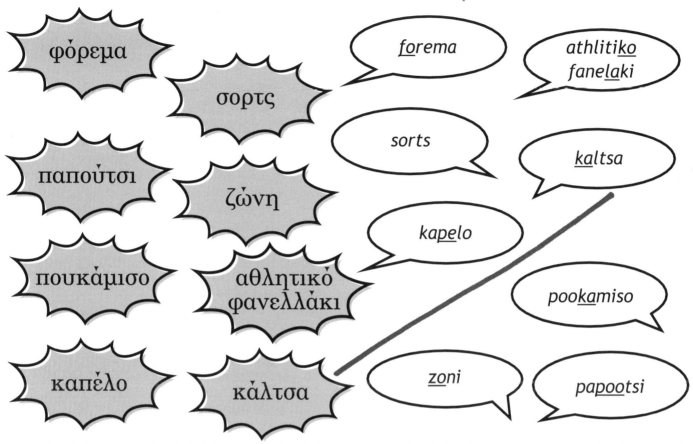

- φόρεμα
- σορτς
- παπούτσι
- ζώνη
- πουκάμισο
- αθλητικό φανελλάκι
- καπέλο
- κάλτσα

- *forema*
- *athlitiko fanelaki*
- *sorts*
- *kaltsa*
- *kapelo*
- *pookamiso*
- *zoni*
- *papootsi*

- -

◎ **S**ee if you can find these clothes in the word square.

The words can run left to right, or top to bottom:

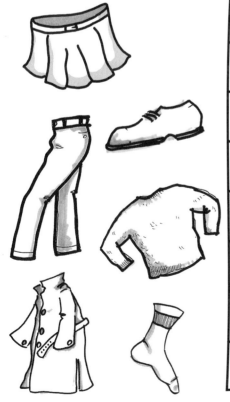

ε	π	α	ν	ω	φ	ό	ρ	ι
π	α	ν	τ	ε	λ	ό	ν	ι
ς	π	ύ	ω	λ	ύ	σ	τ	κ
π	ο	υ	λ	ό	β	ε	ρ	ά
ω	ύ	ν	δ	ψ	σ	υ	ω	λ
ι	τ	η	ρ	π	φ	α	β	τ
ε	σ	τ	ω	σ	δ	ς	ε	σ
λ	ι	κ	φ	ο	ύ	σ	τ	α

Now match the Greek words, their pronunciation, and the English meaning, as in the example.

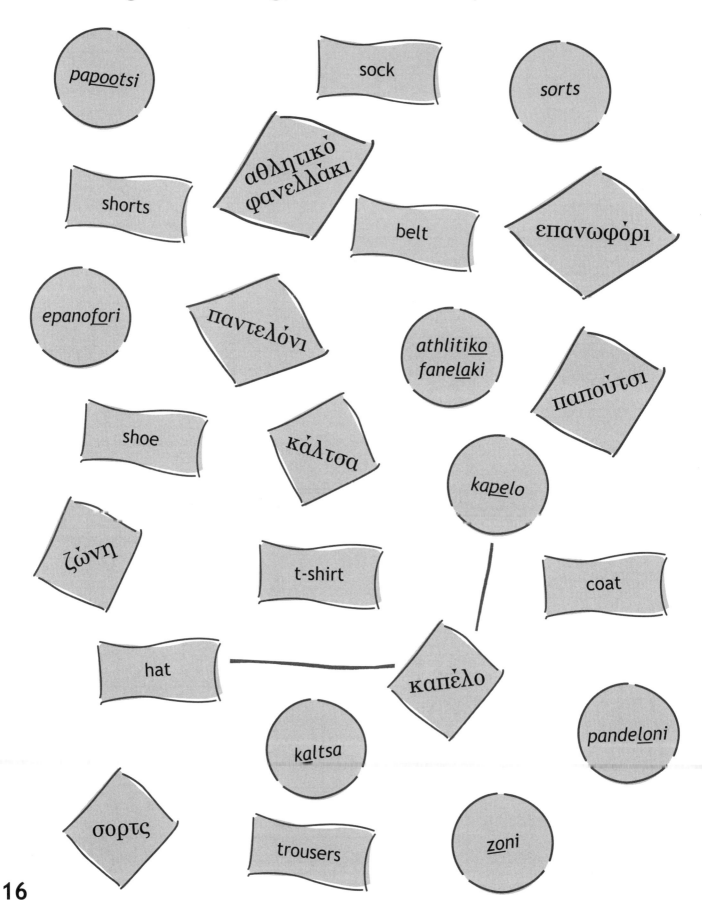

papootsi

sock

sorts

αθλητικό φανελλάκι

shorts

belt

επανωφόρι

epanofori

παντελόνι

athlitiko fanelaki

παπούτσι

shoe

κάλτσα

kapelo

ζώνη

t-shirt

coat

hat

καπέλο

pandeloni

kaltsa

σορτς

trousers

zoni

Candy is going on vacation. Count how many of each type of clothing she is packing in her suitcase.

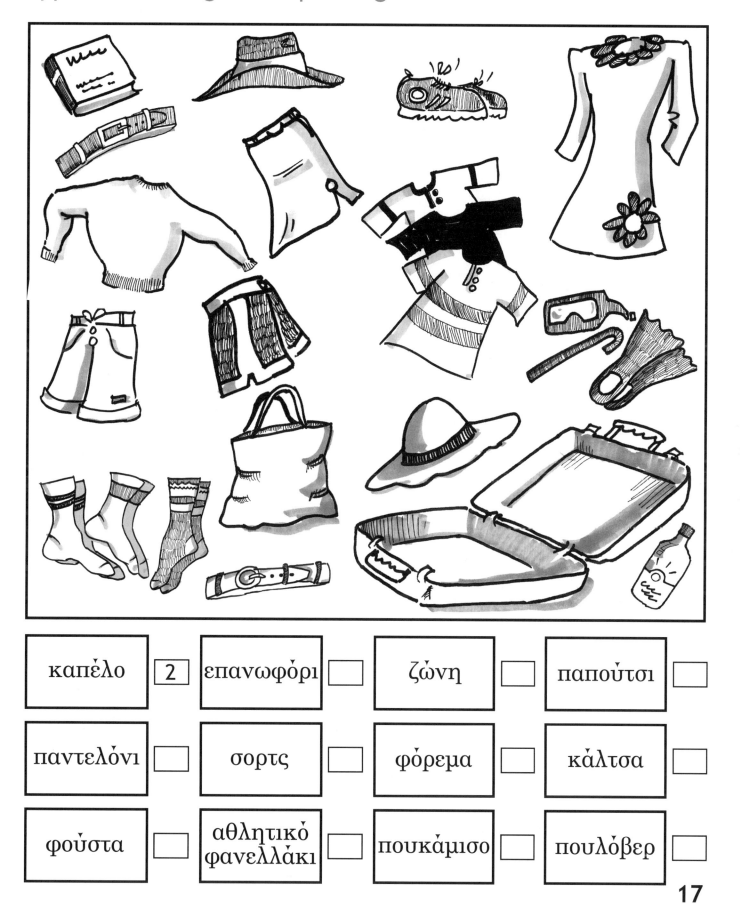

καπέλο	2	επανωφόρι		ζώνη		παπούτσι	
παντελόνι		σορτς		φόρεμα		κάλτσα	
φούστα		αθλητικό φανελλάκι		πουκάμισο		πουλόβερ	

Someone has ripped up the Greek words for clothes.
Can you join the two halves of the words, as in the example?

❸ AROUND TOWN

Look at the pictures of things you might see around town.
Tear out the flashcards for this topic.
Follow steps 1 and 2 of the plan in the introduction.

το ξενοδοχείο
to ksenoTHohio

το λεωφορείο
to leoforio

το σπίτι *to spiti*

το αυτοκίνητο
to aftokinito

το σινεμά
to sinema

το ποδήλατο
to poTHilato

το τρένο
to treno

το ταξί *to taksi*

το σχολείο
to sholio

ο δρόμος
o THromos

το κατάστημα
to katastima

το εστιατόριο
to estiatorio

◎ **M**atch the Greek words to their English equivalents.

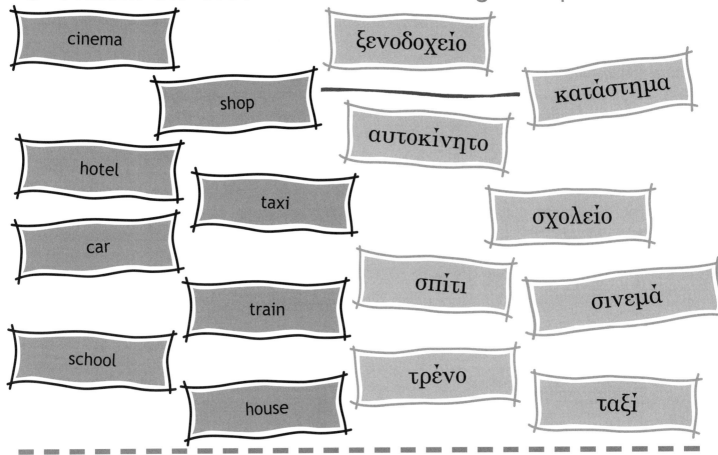

cinema	ξενοδοχείο
shop	κατάστημα
hotel	αυτοκίνητο
taxi	σχολείο
car	σπίτι
train	σινεμά
school	τρένο
house	ταξί

◎ **N**ow put the English words in the same order as the Greek word chain, as in the example.

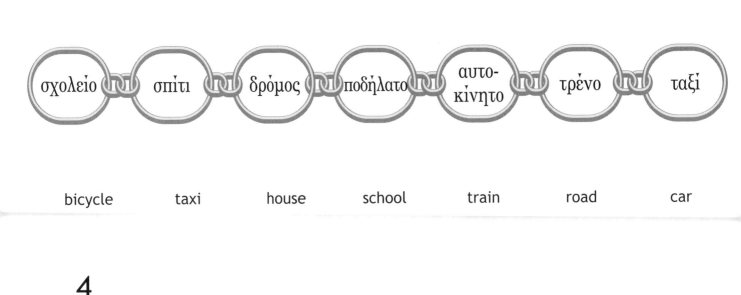

σχολείο — σπίτι — δρόμος — ποδήλατο — αυτο-κίνητο — τρένο — ταξί

bicycle   taxi   house   school   train   road   car

<u>4</u> ___ ___ ___ ___ ___ ___

σχολείο   αυτοκίνητο   ποδήλατο   λεωφορείο

εστιατόριο   τρένο   ξενοδοχείο   ταξί

Now choose the Greek word that matches the picture to fill in the English word at the bottom of the page.

ταξί ⓒ	αυτο-κίνητο ⓕ	σπίτι ⓢ
δρόμος ⓒ	σχολείο ⓐ	ταξί ⓚ
τρένο ⓗ	αυτο-κίνητο ⓔ	δρόμος ⓤ
σπίτι ⓑ	ποδήλατο ⓞ	τρένο ⓦ
σχολείο ⓞ	δρόμος ⓗ	ποδήλατο ⓢ
σπίτι ⓡ	δρόμος ⓖ	σινεμά ⓛ

English word: ⓢ ◯ ◯ ◯ ◯ ◯

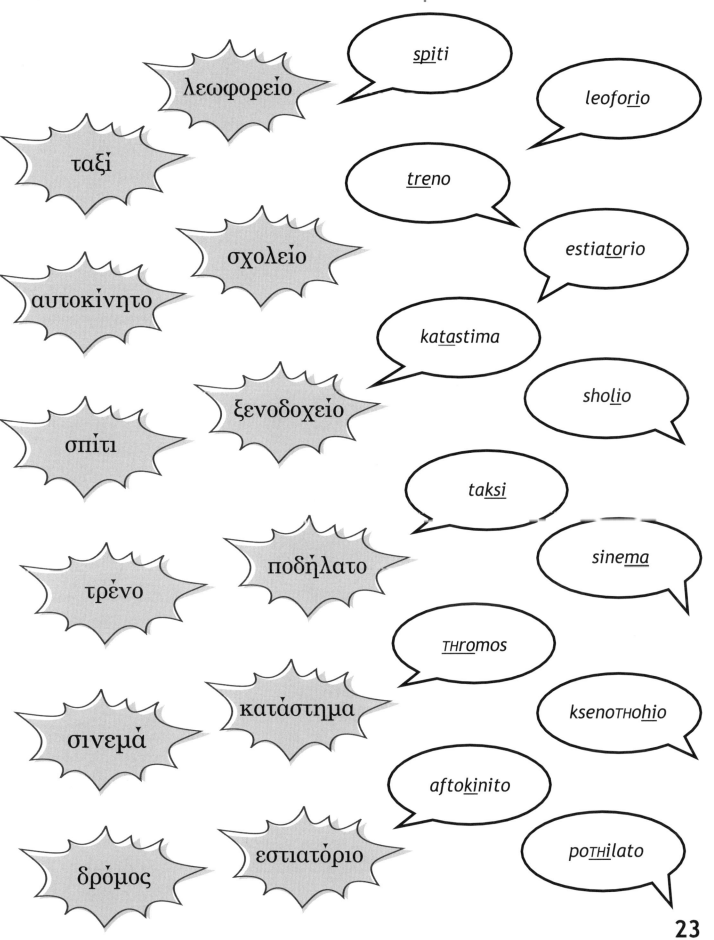

4 COUNTRYSIDE

Look at the pictures of things you might find in the countryside.
Tear out the flashcards for this topic.
Follow steps 1 and 2 of the plan in the introduction.

ο λόφος
o lofos

η γέφυρα
i yefira

το αγρόκτημα
to aghroktima

το βουνό
to voono

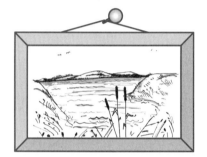

η λίμνη
i limni

το δέντρο
to THendro

το λουλούδι
to loolooTHi

το ποτάμι *to potami*

η θάλασσα
i thalasa

το χωράφι *to horafi*

η έρημος *i erimos*

το δάσος
to THasos

24

Can you match all the countryside words to the pictures.

βουνό

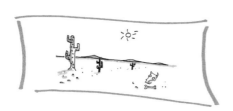 

αγρόκτημα

θάλασσα

δάσος

έρημος

λόφος

λίμνη

γέφυρα

ποτάμι

λουλούδι

δέντρο

χωράφι

Now tick (✔) the features you can find in this landscape.

γέφυρα	✔	δέντρο	☐	έρημος	☐	λόφος	☐
βουνό	☐	θάλασσα	☐	χωράφι	☐	δάσος	☐
λίμνη	☐	ποτάμι	☐	λουλούδι	☐	αγρόκτημα	☐

Match the Greek words and their pronunciation.

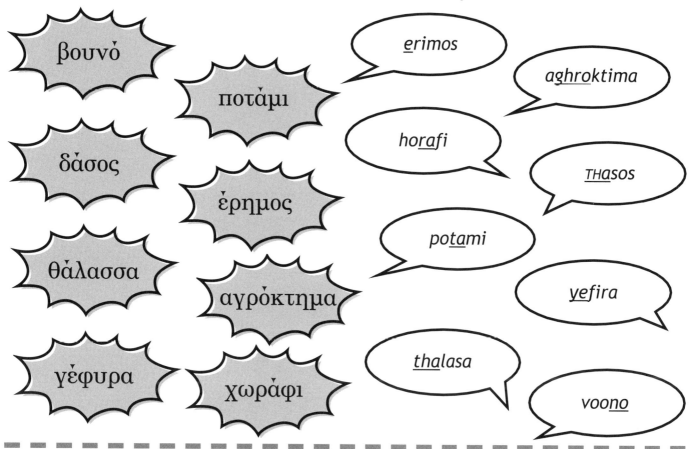

See if you can find these words in the word square.

The words can run left to right, or top to bottom.

δέντρο

αγρόκτημα

λόφος

λουλούδι

γέφυρα

λίμνη

μ	ρ	ψ	λ	τ	υ	χ	κ	ι
γ	ο	ν	α	λ	ό	φ	ο	ς
ε	π	δ	η	υ	τ	ψ	ν	ρ
φ	ς	ε	λ	ι	μ	ν	η	γ
υ	φ	ν	κ	ς	ν	σ	τ	ς
ρ	λ	τ	μ	υ	φ	π	ψ	β
α	γ	ρ	ό	κ	τ	η	μ	α
δ	λ	ο	υ	λ	ο	ύ	δ	ι

© **F**inally, test yourself by joining the Greek words, their pronunciation, and the English meanings, as in the example.

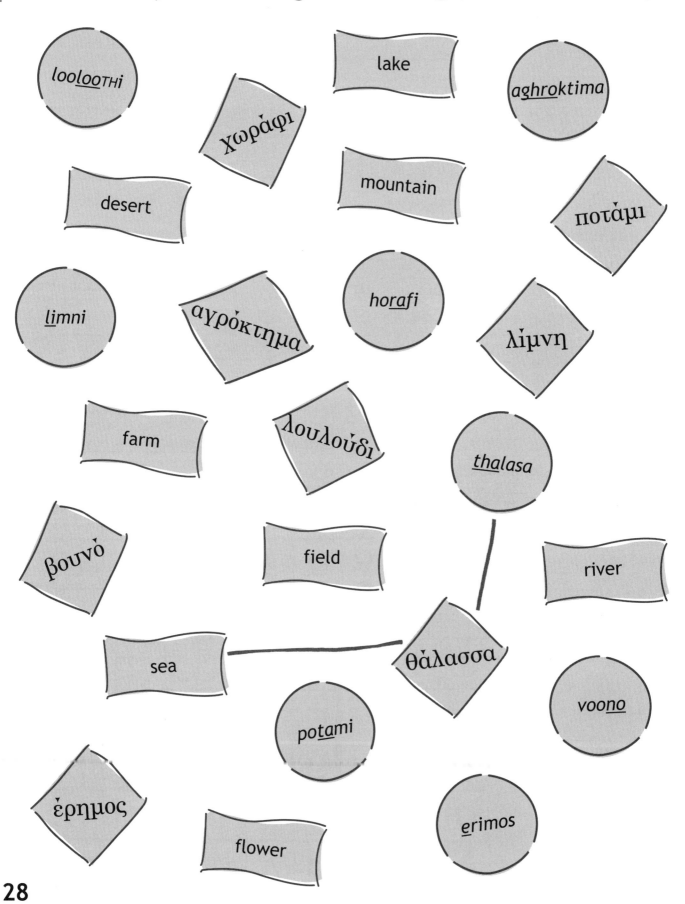

looloothi

lake

aghroktima

Χωράφι

desert

mountain

ποτάμι

limni

αγρόκτημα

horafi

λίμνη

farm

Λουλούδι

thalasa

βουνό

field

river

sea

θάλασσα

voono

potami

έρημος

flower

erimos

⑤ OPPOSITES

Look at the pictures.
Tear out the flashcards for this topic.
Follow steps 1 and 2 of the plan in the introduction.

βρὼμικο
vromiko

καθαρὸ
katharo

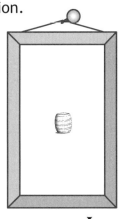

μικρὸ
mikro

μεγὰλο
meghalo

φτηνὸ *ftino*

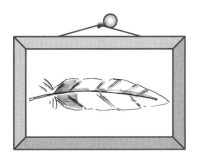

ελαφρὺ *elafri*

αργὸ *argho*

ακριβὸ *akrivo*

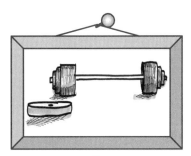

βαρὺ *vari*

γρὴγορο
ghrighoro

παλιὸ *palio*

καινοὺριο
kenoorio

Join the Greek words to their English equivalents.

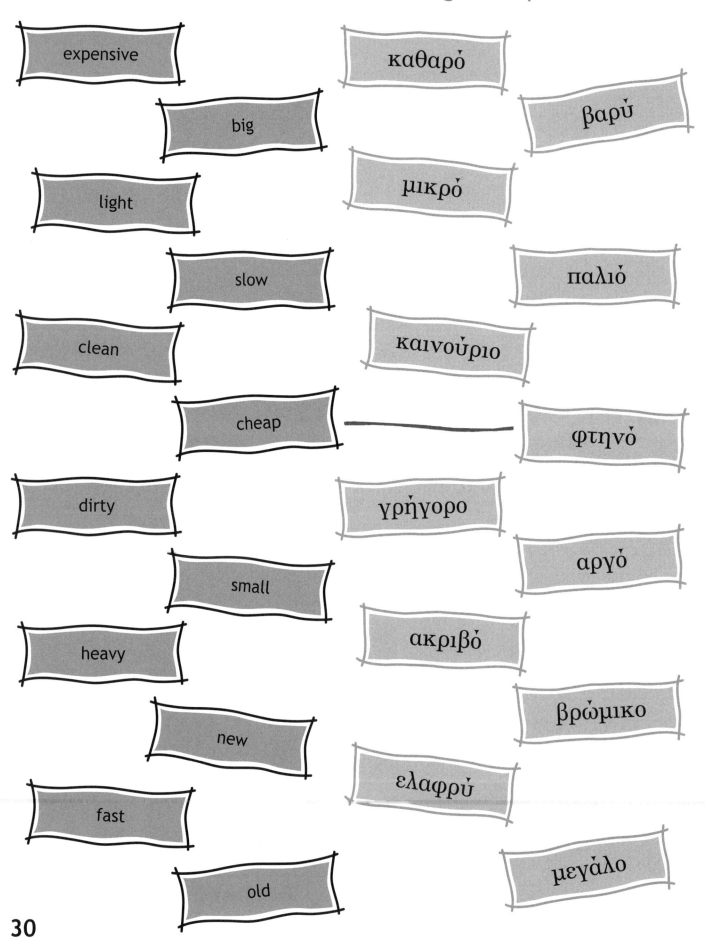

English	Greek
expensive	καθαρό
big	βαρύ
light	μικρό
slow	παλιό
clean	καινούριο
cheap	φτηνό
dirty	γρήγορο
small	αργό
heavy	ακριβό
new	βρώμικο
fast	ελαφρύ
old	μεγάλο

Now choose the Greek word that matches the picture to fill in the English word at the bottom of the page.

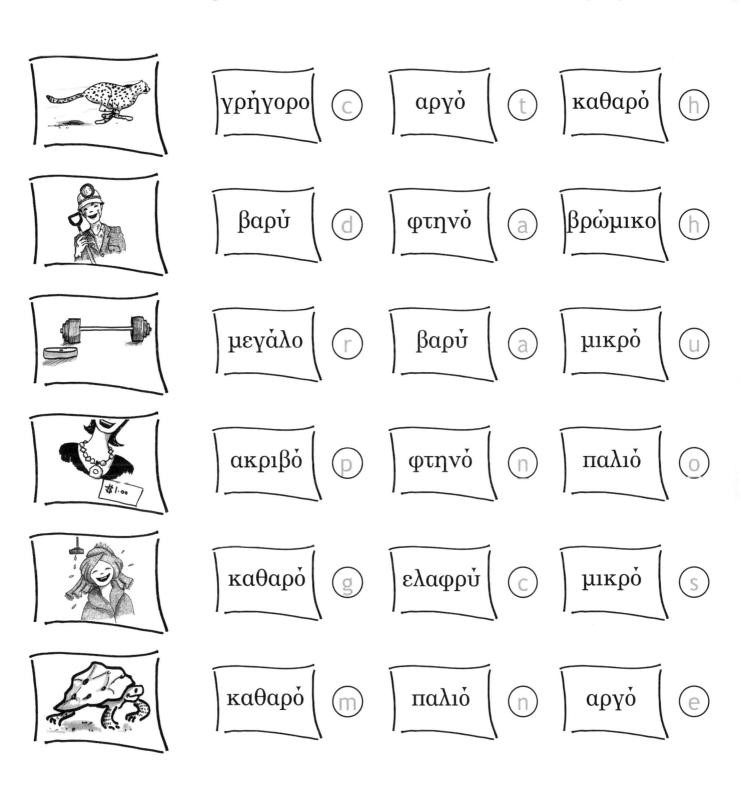

γρήγορο ⓒ	αργό ⓣ	καθαρό ⓗ
βαρύ ⓓ	φτηνό ⓐ	βρώμικο ⓗ
μεγάλο ⓡ	βαρύ ⓐ	μικρό ⓤ
ακριβό ⓟ	φτηνό ⓝ	παλιό ⓞ
καθαρό ⓖ	ελαφρύ ⓒ	μικρό ⓢ
καθαρό ⓜ	παλιό ⓝ	αργό ⓔ

English word:

31

Find the odd one out in these groups of words.

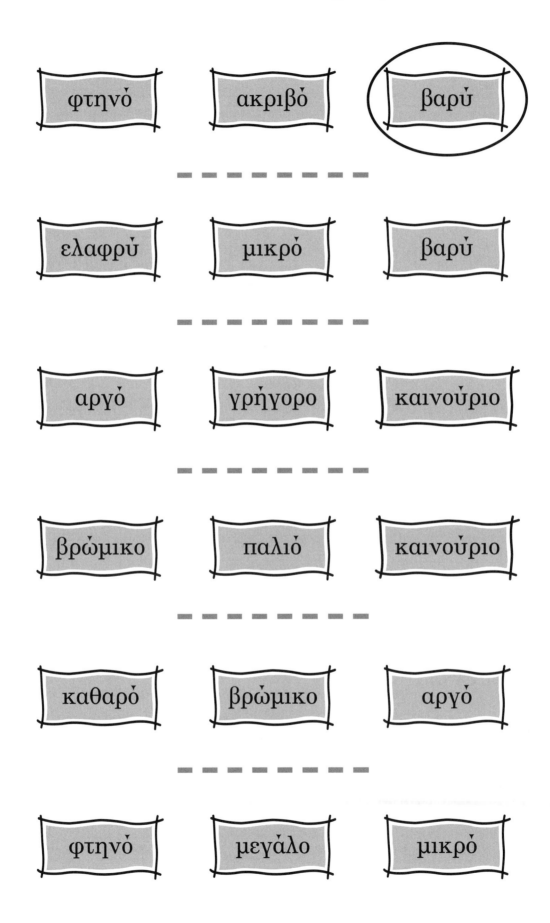

φτηνό ακριβό (βαρύ)

- - - - -

ελαφρύ μικρό βαρύ

- - - - -

αργό γρήγορο καινούριο

- - - - -

βρώμικο παλιό καινούριο

- - - - -

καθαρό βρώμικο αργό

- - - - -

φτηνό μεγάλο μικρό

Finally, join the English words to their Greek opposites, as in the example.

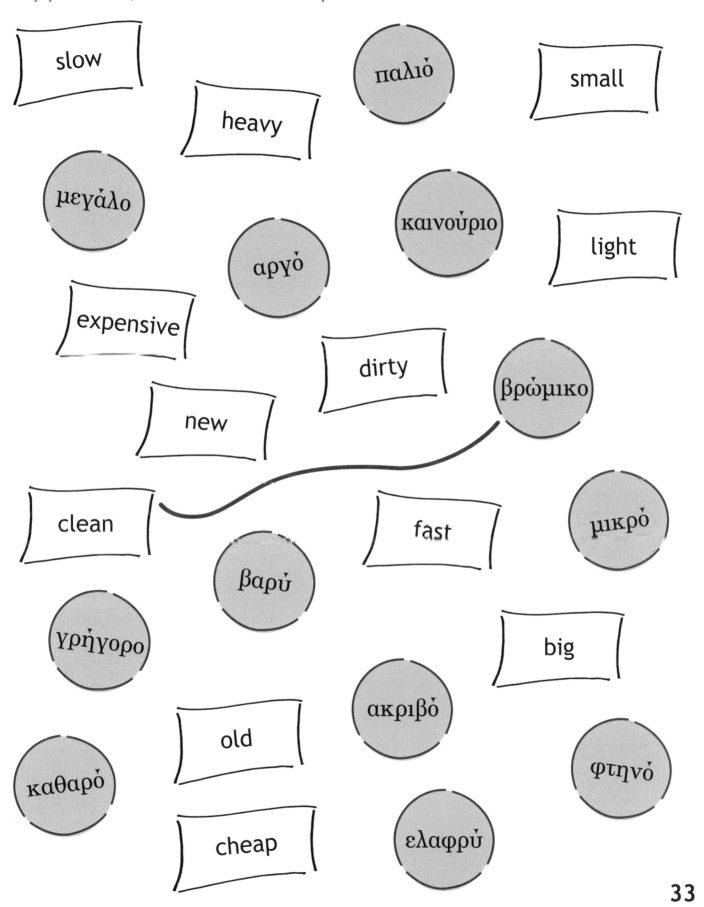

slow

παλιό

small

heavy

μεγάλο

καινούριο

light

αργό

expensive

dirty

βρώμικο

new

clean

fast

μικρό

βαρύ

γρήγορο

big

ακριβό

old

φτηνό

καθαρό

cheap

ελαφρύ

33

⑥ ANIMALS

Look at the pictures.
Tear out the flashcards for this topic.
Follow steps 1 and 2 of the plan in the introduction.

η πάπια *i papia*

ο ελέφαντας
o elefandas

η γάτα
i ghata

ο σκύλος
o skilos

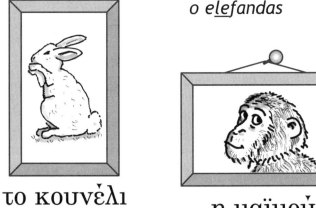

το κουνέλι
to kooneli

η μαϊμού
i maimoo

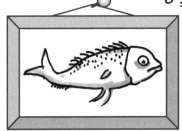

το ψάρι *to psari*

το πρόβατο *to provato*

το ποντίκι
to pondiki

η αγελάδα
i ayelaтна

το άλογο
to alogho

το λεοντάρι
to leondari

34

Match the animals to their associated pictures, as in the example.

κουνέλι

άλογο

μαϊμού

γάτα

πρόβατο

ποντίκι

σκύλος

λεοντάρι

ψάρι

αγελάδα

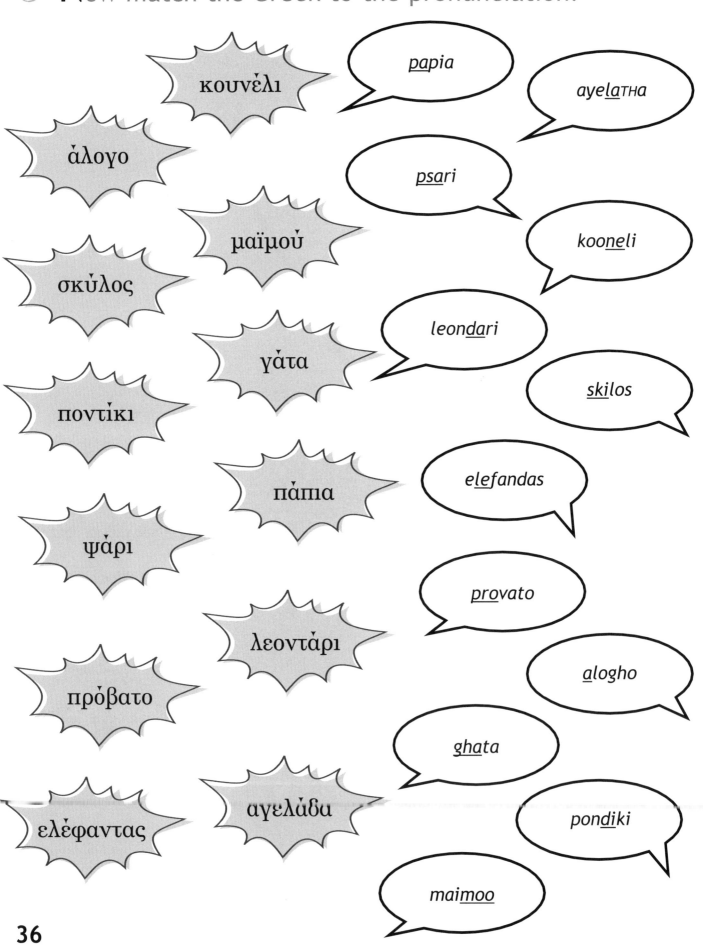

◎ **T**ick (✔) the animal words you can find in the word pile.

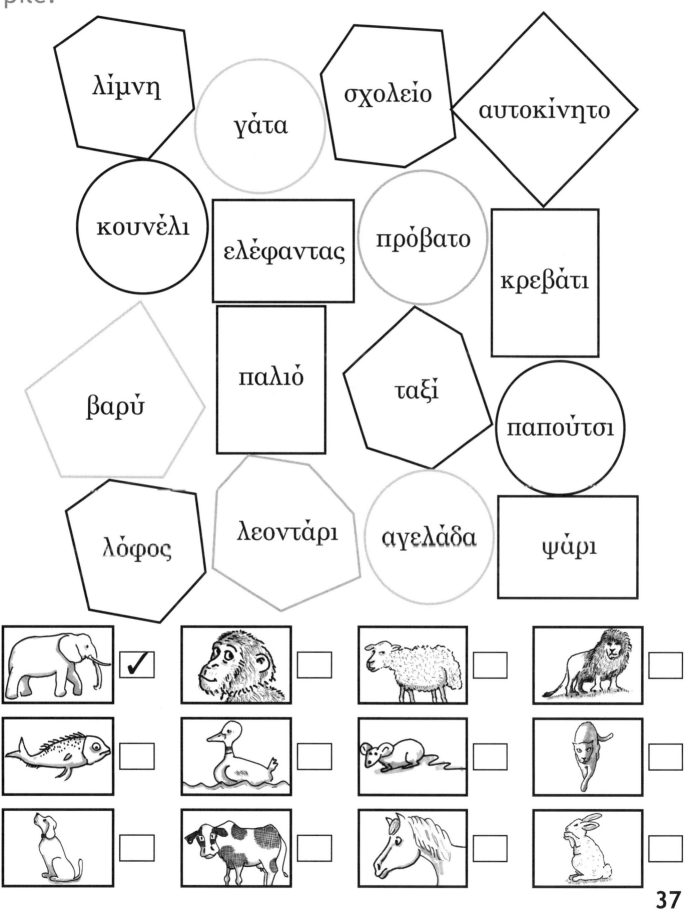

λίμνη

γάτα

σχολείο

αυτοκίνητο

κουνέλι

ελέφαντας

πρόβατο

κρεβάτι

βαρύ

παλιό

ταξί

παπούτσι

λόφος

λεοντάρι

αγελάδα

ψάρι

Join the Greek animals to their English equivalents.

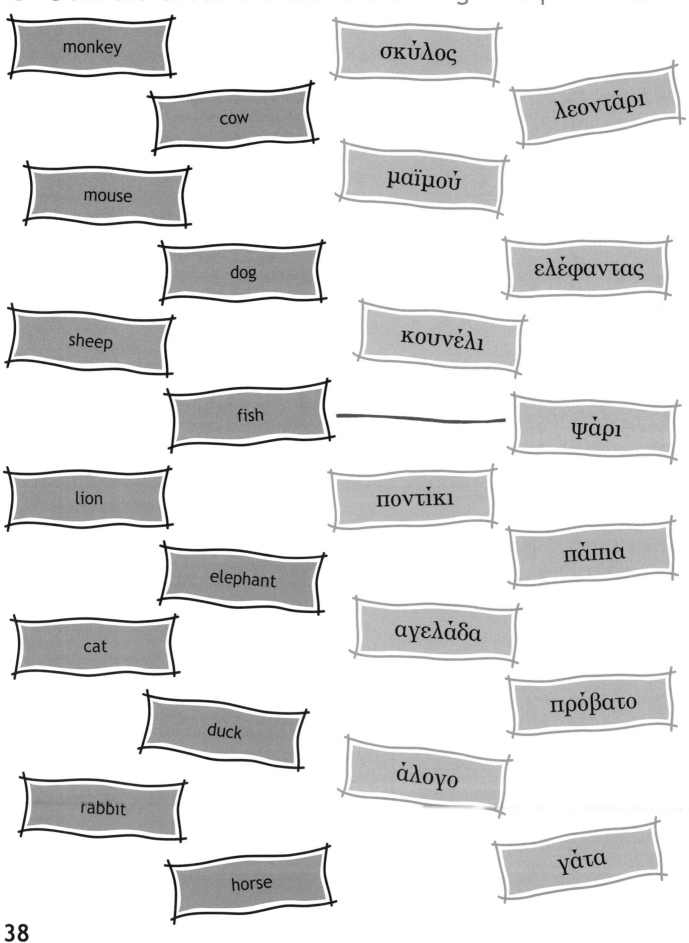

monkey

σκύλος

λεοντάρι

cow

μαϊμού

mouse

dog

ελέφαντας

sheep

κουνέλι

fish ——————— ψάρι

ποντίκι

lion

πάπια

elephant

αγελάδα

cat

πρόβατο

duck

άλογο

rabbit

γάτα

horse

38

❼ PARTS OF THE BODY

Look at the pictures of parts of the body.
Tear out the flashcards for this topic.
Follow steps 1 and 2 of the plan in the introduction.

το δάχτυλο
to тнаhtilo

το κεφάλι
to kefali

ο βραχίονας
o vrahionas

το μάτι   *to mati*

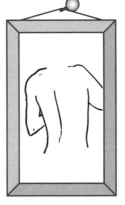

η πλάτη
i plati

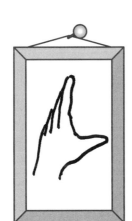

το χέρι
to heri

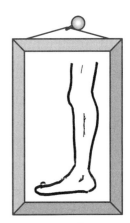

το πόδι
to pотнi

το στομάχι
to stomahi

τα μαλλιά   *ta malia*

το στόμα
to stoma

το αυτί   *to afti*

η μύτη   *i miti*

39

Someone has ripped up the Greek words for parts of the body. Can you join the two halves of the word again?

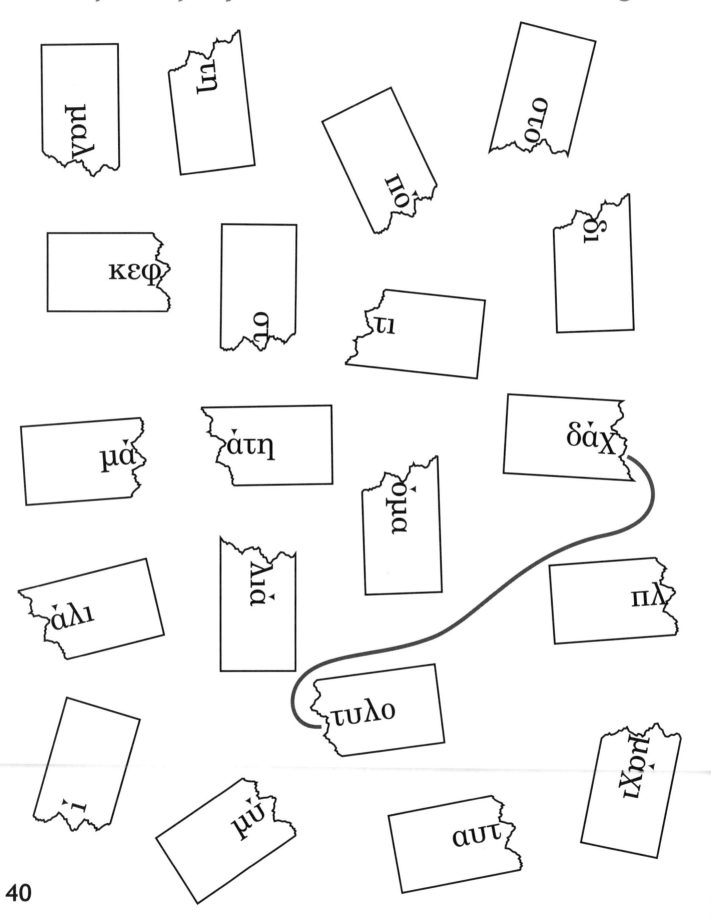

See if you can find and circle six parts of the body in the word square, then draw them in the boxes below.

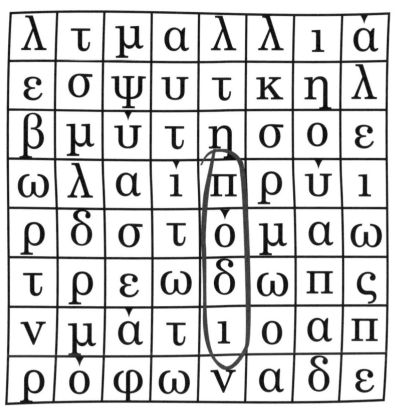

The words can run left to right, or top to bottom:

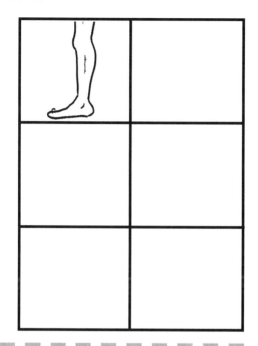

Now match the Greek to the pronunciation.

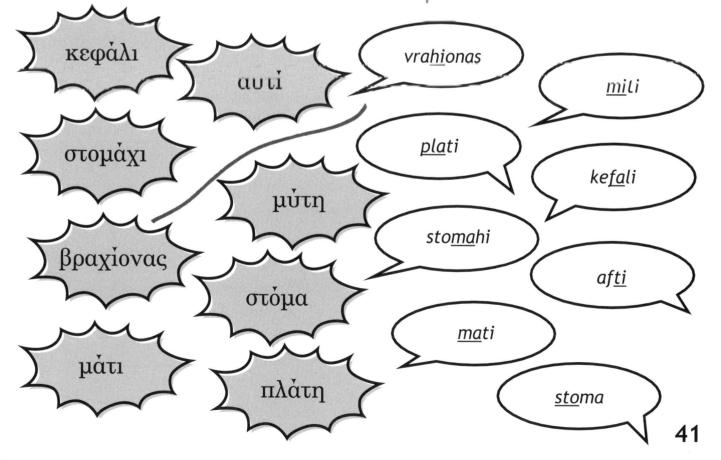

κεφάλι

αυτί

vrahionas

mili

στομάχι

plati

kefali

μύτη

stomahi

βραχίονας

afti

στόμα

mati

μάτι

πλάτη

stoma

41

Label the body with the correct number, and write the pronunciation next to the words.

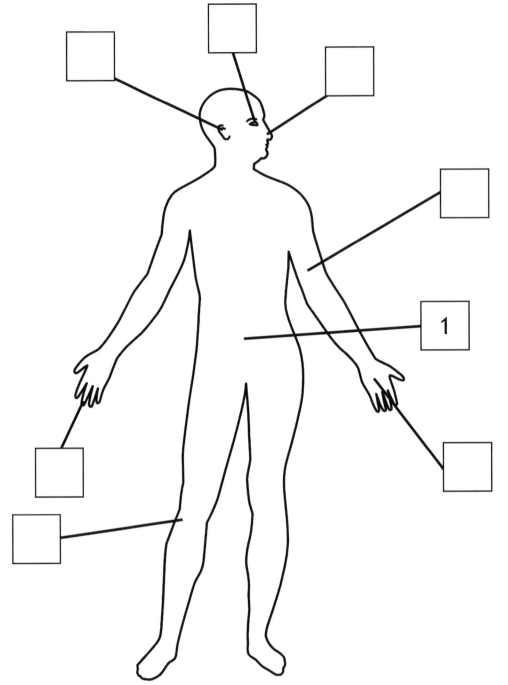

1 στομάχι *stomahi*

2 βραχίονας _____

3 μύτη _____

4 χέρι _____

5 αυτί _____

6 πόδι _____

7 μάτι _____

8 δάχτυλο _____

○ **F**inally, match the Greek words, their pronunciation, and the English meanings, as in the example.

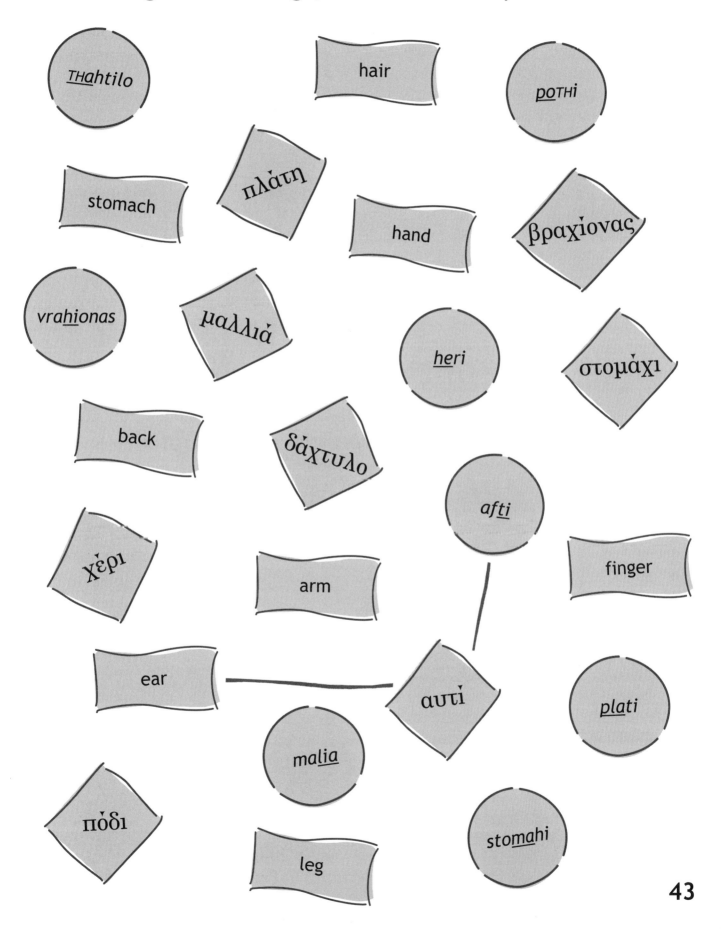

THahtilo

hair

poTHi

stomach

πλάτη

hand

βραχίονας

vrahionas

μαλλιά

heri

στομάχι

back

δάχτυλο

afti

χέρι

arm

finger

ear

αυτί

plati

malia

πόδι

stomahi

leg

43

8 USEFUL EXPRESSIONS

Look at the pictures.
Tear out the flashcards for this topic.
Follow steps 1 and 2 of the plan in the introduction.

πού; *poo?*

όχι *ohi*

ναι *ne*

γειά σου
ya soo

αντίο *andio*

χθες *hthes*

σήμερα *simera*

αύριο *avrio*

εδώ
eTHO

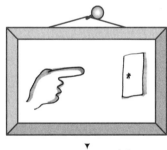

εκεί *eki*

τώρα *tora*

πόσο; *poso?*

συγγνώμη
sighnomi

υπέροχα!
iperoha!

παρακαλώ
parakalo

ευχαριστώ
efharisto

Match the Greek words to their English equivalents.

great!

χθες

ναι

yes

εδώ

yesterday

where?

υπέροχα!

today

παρακαλώ

όχι

here

please

σήμερα

no

πού;

Now match the Greek to the pronunciation.

εκεί

γειά σου

ya soo

andio

αύριο

αντίο

efharisto

iperoha!

πόσο;

ευχαριστώ

avrio

sighnomi

συγγνώμη

υπέροχα!

poso?

eki

45

Choose the Greek word that matches the picture to fill in the English word at the bottom of the page.

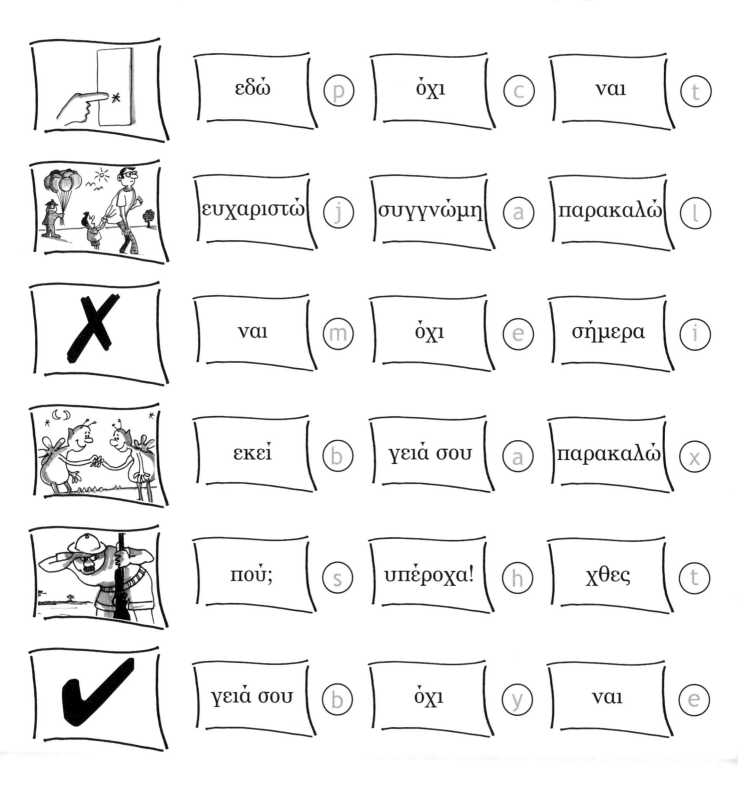

εδώ (p)	ὀχι (c)	ναι (t)
ευχαριστῶ (j)	συγγνώμη (a)	παρακαλῶ (l)
ναι (m)	ὀχι (e)	σήμερα (i)
εκεῖ (b)	γειά σου (a)	παρακαλῶ (x)
πού; (s)	υπέροχα! (h)	χθες (t)
γειά σου (b)	ὀχι (y)	ναι (e)

English word: (p) ( ) ( ) ( ) ( ) ( )

What are these people saying? Write the correct number in each speech bubble, as in the example.

1. γειά σου   2. παρακαλώ   3. ναι   4. όχι

5. εδώ   6. συγγνώμη   7. πού;   8. πόσο;

Finally, match the Greek words, their pronunciation, and the English meanings, as in the example.

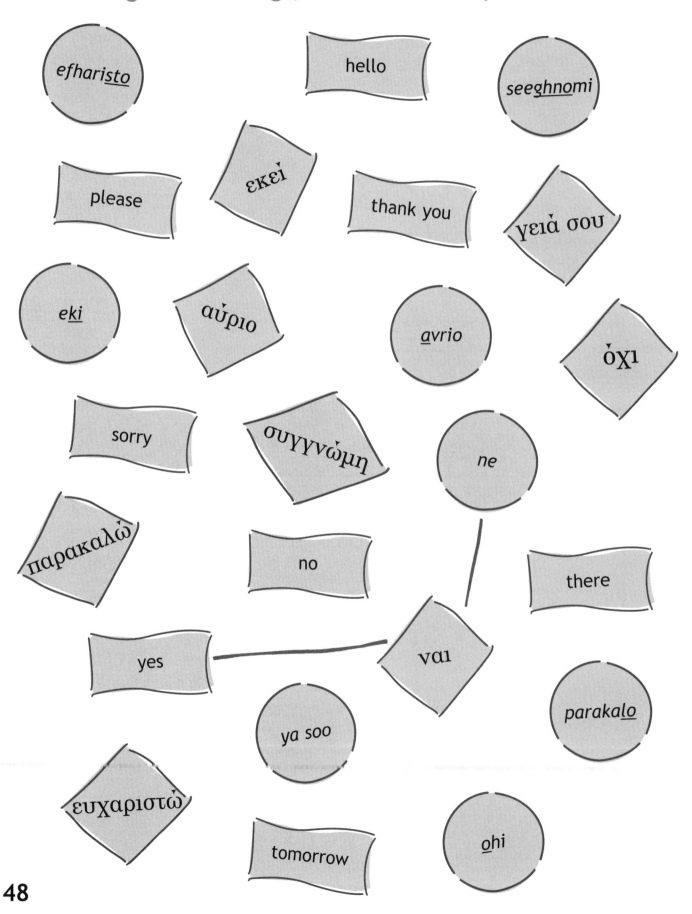

efharisto

hello

seeghnomi

εκεί

please

thank you

γειά σου

eki

αύριο

avrio

όχι

sorry

συγγνώμη

ne

παρακαλώ

no

there

yes

ναι

parakalo

ya soo

ευχαριστώ

tomorrow

ohi

● ROUND-UP

This section is designed to review all the 100 words you have met in the different topics. It is a good idea to test yourself with your flashcards before trying this section.

◎ **T**hese ten objects are hidden in the picture. Can you find and circle them?

πόρτα   λουλούδι   κρεβάτι   επανωφόρι   καπέλο

ποδήλατο   καρέκλα   σκύλος   ψάρι   κάλτσα

© **S**ee if you can remember all these words.

σήμερα

λεωφορείο

γρήγορο

μύτη

έρημος

ναι

ντουλάπι

λεοντάρι

φόρεμα

φτηνό

ποτάμι

πόδι

◎ **F**ind the odd one out in these groups of words and say why.

σκύλος	αγελάδα	(τραπέζι)	μαϊμού

Because it isn't an animal.

αυτοκίνητο	λεωφορείο	τρένο	τηλέφωνο

αυτοκίνητο	επανωφόρι	πουκάμισο	φούστα

θάλασσα	λίμνη	ποτάμι	δέντρο

ακριβό	βρώμικο	καθαρό	σινεμά

κουνέλι	γάτα	ψάρι	λεοντάρι

βραχίονας	καναπές	κεφάλι	στομάχι

παρακαλώ	χθες	αύριο	σήμερα

φούρνος	κρεβάτι	ντουλάπι	ψυγείο

◎ **L**ook at the objects below for 30 seconds.

◎ **C**over the picture and try to remember all the objects.
Circle the Greek words for those you remember.

λουλούδι   παπούτσι   ευχαριστώ   πόρτα

αυτοκίνητο   εδώ   επανωφόρι   τρένο

όχι

ζώνη   βουνό   καρέκλα   άλογο

κάλτσα   μάτι   κρεβάτι

αθλητικό
φανελλάκι

σορτς   ταξί   τηλεόραση   μαϊμού

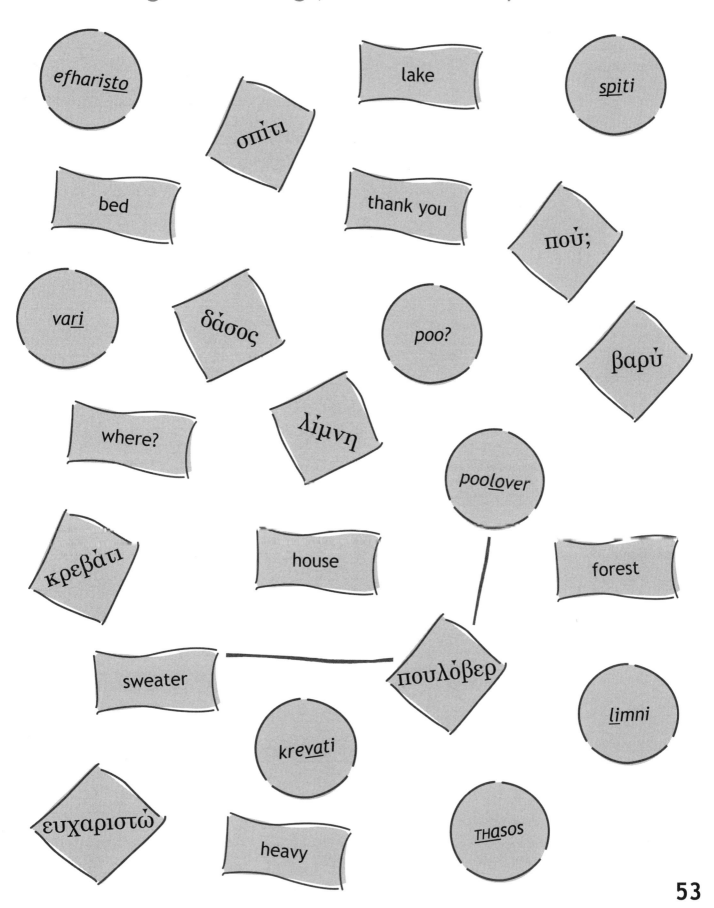

efharisto

lake

spiti

σπὶτι

bed

thank you

πού;

vari

δάσος

poo?

βαρὺ

where?

λίμνη

poolover

κρεβάτι

house

forest

sweater

πουλόβερ

limni

krevati

ευχαριστῶ

heavy

THasos

53

καναπές (w)	ταξὶ (g)	αυτὶ (t)
πάπια (o)	βρώμικο (a)	γέφυρα (e)
ναι (m)	πόσο; (l)	σήμερα (i)
αγελάδα (b)	παράθυρο (l)	κάλτσα (h)
πού; (e)	στόμα (a)	σκύλος (d)
μάτι (o)	τραπέζι (p)	γειά σου (v)
λόφος (n)	όχι (y)	ποτάμι (r)
κουνέλι (n)	δρόμος (e)	φούρνος (s)

English phrase: (w) ◯ ◯ ◯ ◯ ◯ ◯ ◯ !

Look at the two pictures and tick (✔) the objects that are different in Picture B.

Picture A

Picture B

σορτς ☐

αθλητικό φανελλάκι ☐

πόρτα ☐

γάτα ☐

καρέκλα ☐

ψάρι ☐

κάλτσα ☐

σκύλος ☐

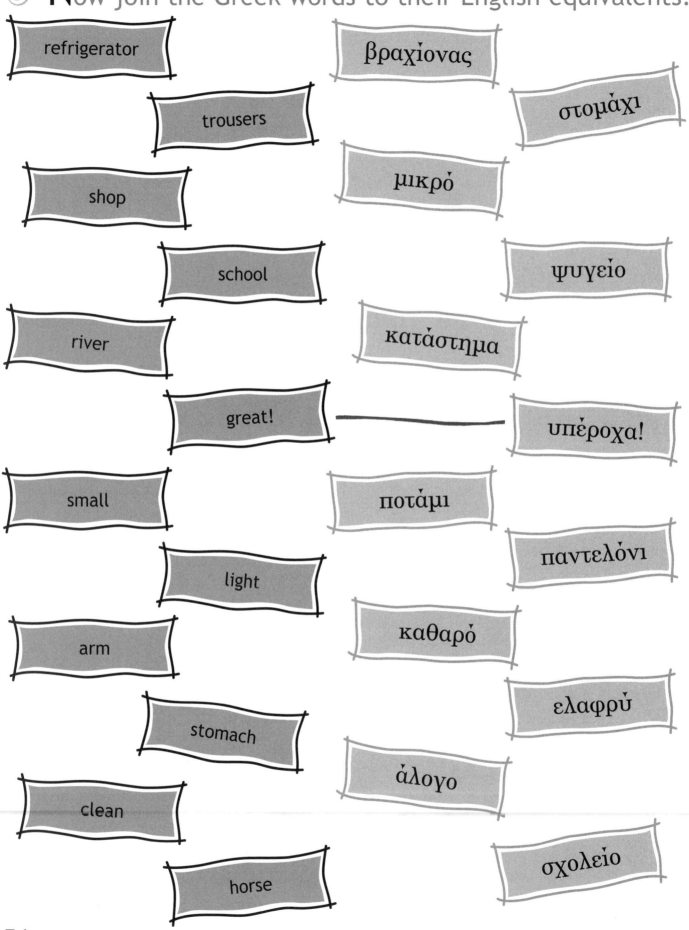

refrigerator

trousers

shop

school

river

great! ———— υπέροχα!

small

light

arm

stomach

clean

horse

βραχίονας

στομάχι

μικρό

ψυγείο

κατάστημα

ποτάμι

παντελόνι

καθαρό

ελαφρύ

άλογο

σχολείο

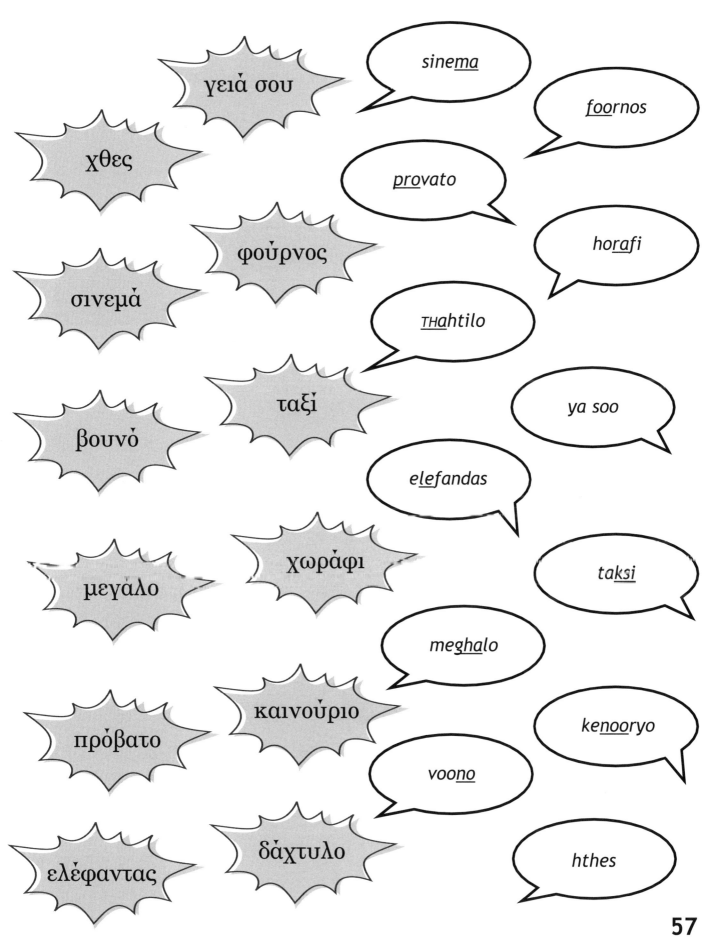

◎ Snake game.

● You will need a die and counter(s). You can challenge yourself to reach the finish or play with someone else. You have to throw the exact number to finish.

● Throw the die and move forward that number of spaces. When you land on a word you must pronounce it and say what it means in English. If you can't, you have to go back to the square you came from.

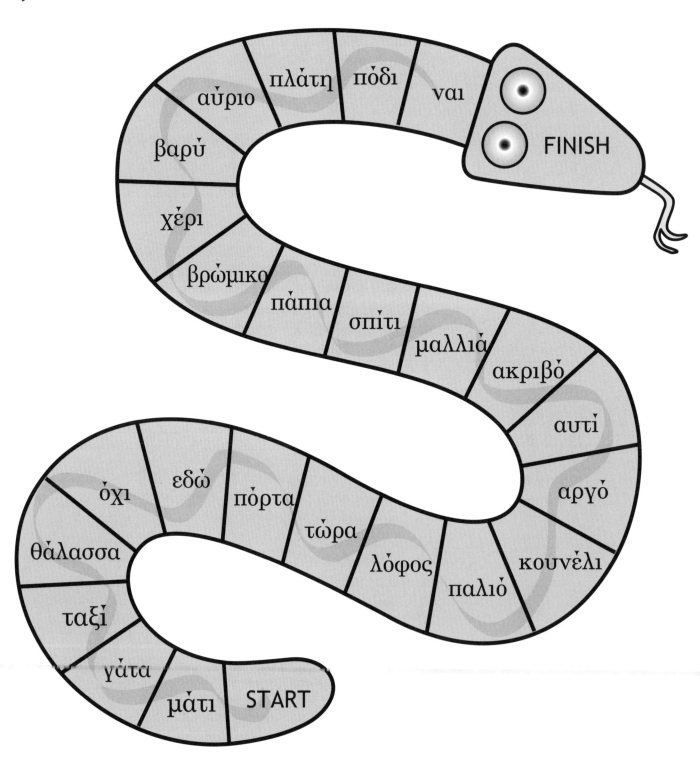

Ⓐ Answers

❶ Around the home

Page 10 (top)
See page 9 for correct picture.

Page 10 (bottom)

door	πόρτα
cupboard	ντουλάπι
stove	φούρνος
bed	κρεβάτι
table	τραπέζι
chair	καρέκλα
refrigerator	ψυγείο
computer	υπολογιστής

Page 11 (top)

τραπέζι	trapezi
ντουλάπι	doolapi
υπολογιστής	ipologhistis
κρεβάτι	krevati
παράθυρο	parathiro
τηλέφωνο	tilefono
τηλεόραση	tileorasi
καρέκλα	karekla

Page 11 (bottom)

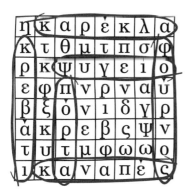

Page 12

Page 13
English word: window

❷ Clothes

Page 15 (top)

φόρεμα	forema
σορτς	sorts
παπούτσι	papootsi
ζώνη	zoni
πουκάμισο	pookamiso
αθλητικό φανελλάκι	athlitiko fanelaki
καπέλο	kapelo
κάλτσα	kaltsa

Page 15 (bottom)

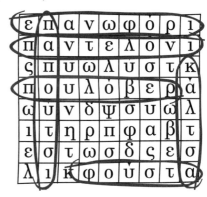

Page 16

hat	καπέλο	kapelo
shoe	παπούτσι	papootsi
sock	κάλτσα	kaltsa
shorts	σορτς	sorts
t-shirt	αθλητικό φανελλάκι	athlitiko fanelaki
belt	ζώνη	zoni
coat	επανωφόρι	epanofori
trousers	παντελόνι	pandeloni

Page 17

καπέλο (hat)	2
επανωφόρι (coat)	0
ζώνη (belt)	2
παπούτσι (shoe)	2 (1 pair)
παντελόνι (trousers)	0
σορτς (shorts)	2
φόρεμα (dress)	1
κάλτσα (sock)	6 (3 pairs)
φούστα (skirt)	1
αθλητικό φανελλάκι (t-shirt)	3
πουκάμισο (shirt)	0
πουλόβερ (sweater)	1

Page 18

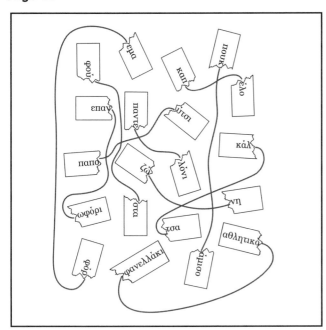

❸ AROUND TOWN

Page 20 (top)

cinema	σινεμά
shop	κατάστημα
hotel	ξενοδοχείο
taxi	ταξί
car	αυτοκίνητο
train	τρένο
school	σχολείο
house	σπίτι

Page 20 (bottom)

bicycle	4
taxi	7
house	2
school	1
train	6
road	3
car	5

Page 21

σχολείο   ταξί   λεωφορείο

αυτοκίνητο   τρένο   εστιατόριο

ξενοδοχείο   ποδήλατο

Page 22

English word: school

Page 23

λεωφορείο	*leofo<u>ri</u>o*
ταξί	*tak<u>si</u>*
σχολείο	*sho<u>li</u>o*
αυτοκίνητο	*afto<u>ki</u>nito*
ξενοδοχείο	*ksenoтно<u>hi</u>o*
σπίτι	*<u>spi</u>ti*
ποδήλατο	*poтн<u>i</u>lato*
τρένο	*<u>tre</u>no*
κατάστημα	*ka<u>ta</u>stima*
σινεμά	*sine<u>ma</u>*
εστιατόριο	*estia<u>to</u>rio*
δρόμος	*тнro<u>mos</u>*

❹ COUNTRYSIDE

Page 25

See page 24 for correct picture.

Page 26

γέφυρα	✔	χωράφι	✔
δέντρο	✔	δάσος	✔
έρημος	✘	λίμνη	✘
λόφος	✘	ποτάμι	✔
βουνό	✔	λουλούδι	✔
θάλασσα	✘	αγρόκτημα	✔

Page 27 (top)

βουνό	*vou<u>no</u>*
ποτάμι	*po<u>ta</u>mi*
δάσος	*тн<u>a</u>sos*
έρημος	*<u>e</u>rimos*
θάλασσα	*<u>tha</u>lasa*
αγρόκτημα	*a<u>ghro</u>ktima*
γέφυρα	*<u>ye</u>fira*
χωράφι	*ho<u>ra</u>fi*

Page 27 (bottom)

μ	ρ	ψ	λ	τ	υ	χ	κ	ι
γ	ο	ν	α	λ	ο	φ	ο	ς
ε	π	δ	η	υ	τ	ψ	ν	ρ
φ	ς	ε	λ	ι	μ	ν	η	γ
υ	φ	ν	κ	ς	ν	ο	τ	ς
ρ	λ	τ	μ	μ	φ	π	ψ	β
α	γ	ρ	ο	κ	τ	ω	μ	α
δ	λ	ο	υ	λ	ο	υ	δ	ι

Page 28

sea	θάλασσα	_thalasa_
lake	λίμνη	_limni_
desert	έρημος	_erimos_
farm	αγρόκτημα	_aghroktima_
flower	λουλούδι	_loolooтнi_
mountain	βουνό	_voono_
river	ποτάμι	_potami_
field	χωράφι	_horafi_

❺ OPPOSITES

Page 30

expensive	ακριβό
big	μεγάλο
light	ελαφρύ
slow	αργό
clean	καθαρό
cheap	φτηνό
dirty	βρώμικο
small	μικρό
heavy	βαρύ
new	καινούριο
fast	γρήγορο
old	παλιό

Page 31
English word: change

Page 32
Odd one outs are those which are not opposites:
βαρύ
μικρό
καινούριο
βρώμικο
αργό
φτηνό

Page 33

old	καινούριο
big	μικρό
new	παλιό
slow	γρήγορο
dirty	καθαρό
small	μεγάλο
heavy	ελαφρύ
clean	βρώμικο
light	βαρύ
expensive	φτηνό
cheap	ακριβό

❻ ANIMALS

Page 35

αγελάδα   κουνέλι   ψάρι

λεοντάρι

πρόβατο   σκύλος   μαϊμού

άλογο   ποντίκι   γάτα

Page 36

κουνέλι	_kooneli_
άλογο	_alogho_
μαιμού	_maimoo_
υκύλος	_skilos_
γάτα	_ghata_
ποντίκι	_pondiki_
πάπια	_papia_
ψάρι	_psari_
λεοντάρι	_leondari_
πρόβατο	_provato_
αγελάδα	_ayelaтнa_
ελέφαντας	_elefandas_

Page 37

elephant	✔	mouse	✘
monkey	✘	cat	✔
sheep	✔	dog	✘
lion	✔	cow	✔
fish	✔	horse	✘
duck	✘	rabbit	✔

Page 38

monkey	μαϊμού
cow	αγελάδα
mouse	ποντίκι
dog	σκύλος
sheep	πρόβατο
fish	ψάρι
lion	λεοντάρι
elephant	ελέφαντας
cat	γάτα
duck	πάπια
rabbit	κουνέλι
horse	άλογο

❼ PARTS OF THE BODY

Page 40

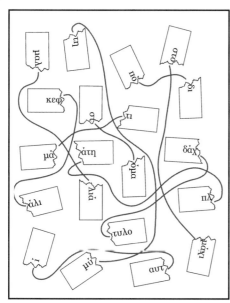

Page 41 (top)

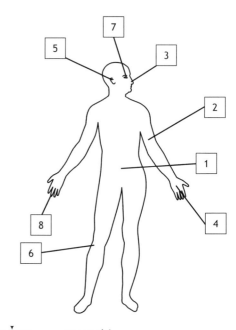

You should have also drawn pictures of:

leg; mouth; ear; nose; eye; hair

Page 41 (bottom)

κεφάλι	*kefali*
αυτί	*afti*
στομάχι	*stomahi*
μύτη	*miti*
βραχίονας	*vrahionas*
στόμα	*stoma*
μάτι	*mati*
πλάτη	*plati*

Page 42

1. στομάχι — *stomahi*
2. βραχίονας — *vrahionas*
3. μύτη — *miti*
4. χέρι — *heri*
5. αυτί — *afti*
6. πόδι — *poThi*
7. μάτι — *mati*
8. δάχτυλο — *THahtilo*

Page 43

ear	αυτί	*afti*
hair	μαλλιά	*malia*
hand	χέρι	*heri*
stomach	στομάχι	*stomahi*
arm	βραχίονας	*vrahionas*
back	πλάτη	*plati*
finger	δάχτυλο	*THahtilo*
leg	πόδι	*poThi*

❽ Useful expressions

Page 45 (top)

great!	υπέροχα!
yes	ναι
yesterday	χθες
where?	πού;
today	σήμερα
here	εδώ
please	παρακαλώ
no	όχι

Page 45 (bottom)

εκεί	_eki_
γειά σου	_ya soo_
αύριο	_avrio_
αντίο	_andio_
πόσο;	_poso?_
ευχαριστώ	_efharisto_
συγγνώμη	_sighnomi_
υπέροχα!	_iperoha!_

Page 46

English word: please

Page 47

Page 48

yes	ναι	_ne_
hello	γειά σου	_ya soo_
no	όχι	_ohi_
sorry	συγγνώμη	_seeghnomi_
please	παρακαλώ	_parakalo_
there	εκεί	_eki_
thank you	ευχαριστώ	_efharisto_
tomorrow	αύριο	_avrio_

⬤ Round-up

Page 49

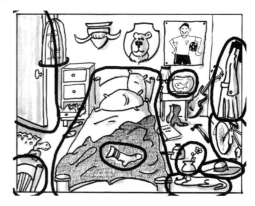

Page 50

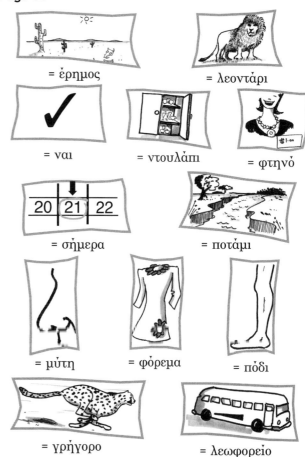

= έρημος

= λεοντάρι

= ναι

= ντουλάπι

= φτηνό

= σήμερα

= ποτάμι

= μύτη

= φόρεμα

= πόδι

= γρήγορο

= λεωφορείο

Page 51

τραπέζι (Because it isn't an animal.)

τηλέφωνο (Because it isn't a means of transportation.)

αγρόκτημα (Because it isn't an item of clothing.)

δέντρο (Because it isn't connected with water.)

σινεμά (Because it isn't a descriptive word.)

ψάρι (Because it lives in water/doesn't have legs.)

καναπές (Because it isn't a part of the body.)

παρακαλώ (Because it isn't an expression of time.)

κρεβάτι (Because you wouldn't find it in the kitchen.)

Page 52

Words that appear in the picture:

αθλητικὸ φανελλάκι
αυτοκίνητο
λουλούδι
παπούτσι
τρένο
μαϊμού
τηλεόραση
καρέκλα
ζώνη
σορτς

Page 53

sweater	πουλόβερ	poolover
lake	λίμνη	limni
thank you	ευχαριστώ	efharisto
bed	κρεβάτι	krevati
house	σπίτι	spiti
forest	δάσος	THasos
where?	πού;	poo?
heavy	βαρύ	vari

Page 54

English phrase: well done!

Page 55

σορτς	✔ (shade)
αθλητικὸ φανελλάκι	✘
πόρτα	✔ (handle)
γάτα	✘
καρέκλα	✔ (back)
ψάρι	✔ (direction)
κάλτσα	✔ (pattern)
σκύλος	✘

Page 56

refrigerator	ψυγείο
trousers	παντελόνι
shop	κατάστημα
school	σχολείο
river	ποτάμι
great!	υπέροχα!
small	μικρό
light	ελαφρύ
arm	βραχίονας
stomach	στομάχι
clean	καθαρό
horse	άλογο

Page 57

γειά σου	ya soo
χθες	hthes
φούρνος	foornos
σινεμά	sinema
ταξί	taksi
βουνό	voono
χωράφι	horafi
μεγάλο	meghalo
καινούριο	kenooryo
πρόβατο	provato
δάχτυλο	THahtilo
ελέφαντας	elefandas

Page 58

Here are the English equivalents of the word, in order from START to FINISH:

eye	mati	ear	afti
cat	ghata	expensive	akrivo
taxi	taksi	hair	malia
sea	thalasa	house	spiti
no	ohi	duck	papia
here	eTHO	dirty	vromiko
door	porta	hand	heri
now	tora	heavy	vari
hill	lofos	tomorrow	avrio
old	palio	back	plati
rabbit	kooneli	leg	poTHi
slow	argho	yes	ne

ο υπολογιστὴς

o ipologhi<u>stis</u>

το παράθυρο

to pa<u>ra</u>thiro

το τραπέζι

to trap<u>e</u>zi

το ντουλάπι

to doo<u>la</u>pi

το ψυγείο

to psi<u>yi</u>o

η καρέκλα

i kar<u>e</u>kla

ο καναπές

o kanap<u>es</u>

ο φούρνος

o <u>foo</u>rnos

η πόρτα

i <u>po</u>rta

το κρεβάτι

to krev<u>a</u>ti

το τηλέφωνο

to ti<u>le</u>fono

η τηλεόραση

i tile<u>o</u>rasi

window	computer
cupboard	table
chair	refrigerator
stove	sofa
bed	door
television	telephone

η ζώνη

i zoni

το επανωφόρι

to epanofori

η φούστα

i foosta

το καπέλο

to kapelo

το αθλητικό φανελλάκι

to athlitiko fanelaki

το παπούτσι

to papootsi

το πουλόβερ

to poolover

το πουκάμισο

to pookamiso

το σορτς

to sorts

η κάλτσα

i kaltsa

το παντελόνι

to pandeloni

το φόρεμα

to forema

coat	belt
hat	skirt
shoe	t-shirt
shirt	sweater
sock	shorts
dress	trousers

το σχολείο

to sholio

το αυτοκίνητο

to aftokinito

ο δρόμος

o ᴛʜromos

το σινεμά

to sinema

το ξενοδοχείο

to ksenoᴛʜohio

το κατάστημα

to katastima

το ταξί

to taksi

το ποδήλατο

to pothilato

το εστιατόριο

to estiatorio

το λεωφορείο

to leoforio

το τρένο

to treno

το σπίτι

to spiti

car	school
cinema	road
shop	hotel
bicycle	taxi
bus	restaurant
house	train

η λὶμνη

i limni

το δὰσος

to THasos

ο λὸφος

o lofos

η θὰλασσα

i thalasa

το βουνὸ

to voono

το δὲντρο

to THendro

η ἐρημος

i erimos

το λουλοὺδι

to loolooTHi

η γὲφυρα

i yefira

το ποτὰμι

to potami

το αγρὸκτημα

to aghroktima

το χωρὰφι

to horafi

forest	lake
sea	hill
tree	mountain
flower	desert
river	bridge
field	farm

βαρὺ

va<u>ri</u>

ελαφρὺ

ela<u>fri</u>

μεγάλο

me<u>gh</u>alo

μικρὸ

mi<u>kro</u>

παλιὸ

pali<u>o</u>

καινούριο

ke<u>noo</u>rio

γρήγορο

<u>gh</u>ri<u>gh</u>oro

αργὸ

ar<u>gho</u>

καθαρὸ

katha<u>ro</u>

βρώμικο

<u>vro</u>miko

φτηνὸ

fti<u>no</u>

ακριβὸ

akri<u>vo</u>

light	heavy
small	big
new	old
slow	fast
dirty	clean
expensive	cheap

η πάπια

i papia

η γάτα

i ghata

το ποντίκι

to pondiki

η αγελάδα

i ayelaτηα

το κουνέλι

to kooneli

ο σκύλος

o skilos

το άλογο

to alogho

η μαϊμού

i maimoo

το λεοντάρι

to leondari

το ψάρι

to psari

ο ελέφαντας

o elefandas

το πρόβατο

to provato

cat	duck
cow	mouse
dog	rabbit
monkey	horse
fish	lion
sheep	elephant

ο βραχίονας

o vrahionas

το δάχτυλο

to THAhtilo

το κεφάλι

to kefali

το στόμα

to stoma

το αυτί

to afti

το πόδι

to poTHi

το χέρι

to heri

το στομάχι

to stomahi

το μάτι

to mati

τα μαλλιά

ta malia

η μύτη

i miti

η πλάτη

i plati

finger	arm
mouth	head
leg	ear
stomach	hand
hair	eye
back	nose

παρακαλώ

parakalo

ευχαριστώ

efharisto

ναι

ne

όχι

ohi

γειά σου

ya soo

αντίο

andio

χθες

hthes

σήμερα

simera

αύριο

avrio

πού;

poo?

εδώ

eTHO

εκεί

eki

συγγνώμη

sighnomi

πόσο;

poso?

υπέροχα!

iperoha!

τώρα

tora

thank you	please
no	yes
goodbye	hello
today	yesterday
where?	tomorrow
there	here
how much?	sorry!
now	great!